A YEAR OF

Questions

A 52-WEEK Q&A BOOK
FOR COUPLES TO COMPLETE TOGETHER, CONNECT,
AND HAVE MEANINGFUL CONVERSATIONS

ASHLEY AND MARCUS KUSI

Join Our Community

To receive updates about future books, courses, workshops and our monthly inspirational newsletter for couples, visit the website below.

www.ourpeacefulfamily.com/bookfan

Contents

Introduction

From our experience, finding new ways to connect with your partner every week can be challenging. Life happens, different schedules, work, and children, etc. However, making time for the two of you should always remain the priority. Specifically, it is best to have one-on-one time with your partner every single day, and then a longer period once per week.

After being together for many years, we have realized that so much of our connection comes from meaningful conversations. As such, we want to share what has worked for us in the hope you and your partner can also receive the gift of emotional intimacy through engaging conversation. That's why we created *A Year of Questions*, a simple activity book to make it easier for you and your partner to add fun conversations and something new to your relationship.

Once a week, sit down with a glass of wine or coffee, and use the thought-provoking questions in this book to help you learn a little bit more about each other. Because that curiosity to always learn something new about your partner is essential to strengthening your bond and growing together as a couple. In other words, you should never stop learning about your partner. Even if you've been together for several years, like we have, there is always something new to discover.

We hope *A Year of Questions* helps you and your partner to connect, have fun and engage in meaningful conversations every week for this next year.

Enjoy!

Ash and Marcus

How to Use This Book

First, decide who will respond as *You* and who will respond as *Me* for the remainder of this book.

You: _____

Me: _____

Second, schedule a day each week to open the book and find a new question to write your answers to. You can do this independently and then read your responses aloud to each other, or you can just verbally explain if that works better for you instead of writing it all out (we won't judge!).

Third, ask each other questions to dive deeper into your answers, and be open with your own responses. See how your answers are similar and different. Explore your partner's history, their views of the world, and what they really think of you.

Four Ways to Get the Most out of Your Weekly Activities

1. Gather supplies.

Grab some yummy snacks and a drink that's delicious. Don't forget a pen!

2. Create the right setting.

Get comfy and settle in. Put your phones and other distractions away.

3. Relax.

Come in with no expectations and an open mind. Explore the questions that pop into your mind as you both listen to each other's responses, and feel free to go off on tangents.

4. Get closer.

Make the most out of this time by keeping eye contact, sitting close, and/or holding hands.

Now, get started on your weekly conversation date by turning the page.

1

I am thankful you...

You:

1. _____
2. _____
3. _____
4. _____
5. _____
6. _____
7. _____
8. _____
9. _____
10. _____

1

I am thankful you...

Me:

1. _____

2. _____

3. _____

4. _____

5. _____

6. _____

7. _____

8. _____

9. _____

10. _____

These experiences taught me about love:

You:

_____

_____

_____

_____

_____

_____

_____

_____

_____

_____

2

These experiences taught me about love:

Me:

_____

_____

_____

_____

_____

_____

_____

_____

_____

3 *Three ways I love helping people are...*

You:

_____

_____

_____

_____

_____

_____

_____

_____

_____

3

Three ways I love helping people are...

Me:

_____

_____

_____

_____

_____

_____

_____

_____

_____

_____

_____

 **What I admire most about my partner is...**

You:

_____

_____

_____

_____

_____

_____

_____

_____

_____

_____

_____

 **What I admire most about my partner is...**

Me:

_____

_____

_____

_____

_____

_____

_____

_____

_____

5

My parents dealt with and talked about money...

You:

_____

_____

_____

_____

_____

_____

_____

_____

_____

_____

_____

5

My parents dealt with and talked about money...

Me:

_____

_____

_____

_____

_____

_____

_____

_____

_____

_____

6

You are really great at...

You:

1. _____

2. _____

3. _____

4. _____

5. _____

6. _____

7. _____

8. _____

9. _____

10. _____

6

You are really great at...

Me:

1. _____

2. _____

3. _____

4. _____

5. _____

6. _____

7. _____

8. _____

9. _____

10. _____

7

This is how I was taught to deal with my emotions growing up:

How I handle emotions now is...

You:

_____

_____

_____

_____

_____

_____

_____

_____

_____

_____

7

This is how I was taught to deal with my emotions growing up:

How I handle emotions now is...

Me:

_____

_____

_____

_____

_____

_____

_____

_____

_____

_____

The types of conversations about our relationship that excite me are...

You:

_____

_____

_____

_____

_____

_____

_____

_____

_____

_____

The types of conversations about our relationship that excite me are...

Me:

_____

_____

_____

_____

_____

_____

_____

_____

_____

_____

9

One thing I liked and one thing that was challenging about my week were...

You:

_____

_____

_____

_____

_____

_____

_____

_____

_____

_____

9

One thing I liked and one thing that was challenging about my week were...

Me:

_____

_____

_____

_____

_____

_____

_____

_____

_____

_____

_____

10

*One thing that would make sex with
you even more amazing is...*

You:

_____

_____

_____

_____

_____

_____

_____

_____

_____

_____

10

*One thing that would make sex with
you even more amazing is...*

Me:

_____

_____

_____

_____

_____

_____

_____

_____

_____

_____

I was _____ when I realized I loved
you for the first time and I felt...

You:

_____

_____

_____

_____

_____

_____

_____

_____

_____

_____

I was _____ when I realized I loved you for the first time and I felt...

Me:

_____

_____

_____

_____

_____

_____

_____

_____

_____

This is how I describe you to other people:

You:

_____

_____

_____

_____

_____

_____

_____

_____

_____

_____

This is how I describe you to other people:

Me:

_____

_____

_____

_____

_____

_____

_____

_____

_____

_____

13

I still can't believe you...

You:

_____

_____

_____

_____

_____

_____

_____

_____

_____

_____

_____

13

I still can't believe you...

Me:

_____

_____

_____

_____

_____

_____

_____

_____

_____

_____

*I feel safe enough to be completely
vulnerable with you about my past and
my current feelings because...*

You:

_____

_____

_____

_____

_____

_____

_____

_____

_____

_____

14

I feel safe enough to be completely vulnerable with you about my past and my current feelings because...

Me:

_____

_____

_____

_____

_____

_____

_____

_____

_____

_____

15

Five personal goals I have that are not related to our relationship are...

You:

1. _____

2. _____

3. _____

4. _____

5. _____

15

Five personal goals I have that are not related to our relationship are...

Me:

1. _____

2. _____

3. _____

4. _____

5. _____

16

This is one of my favorite quotes and why I love it...

You:

_____

_____

_____

_____

_____

_____

_____

_____

_____

_____

_____

16

This is one of my favorite quotes and why I love it...

Me:

_____

_____

_____

_____

_____

_____

_____

_____

_____

_____

_____

17

A difficult experience that involved me letting go was...

You:

_____
_____
_____
_____
_____
_____
_____
_____
_____
_____
_____
_____

17

A difficult experience that involved me letting go was...

Me:

_____

_____

_____

_____

_____

_____

_____

_____

_____

_____

This is what money means to me:

You:

_____

_____

_____

_____

_____

_____

_____

_____

_____

_____

This is what money means to me:

Me:

_____

_____

_____

_____

_____

_____

_____

_____

_____

_____

_____

19

This is how you have challenged me to become better...

You:

_____

_____

_____

_____

_____

_____

_____

_____

_____

_____

_____

19

This is how you have challenged me
to become better...

Me:

_____

_____

_____

_____

_____

_____

_____

_____

_____

_____

_____

_____

An area of my life I would like more of your support in is...

You:

_____

_____

_____

_____

_____

_____

_____

_____

_____

_____

20

*An area of my life I would like
more of your support in is...*

Me:

_____

_____

_____

_____

_____

_____

_____

_____

_____

_____

21

Three things I would like to accomplish with you this year are:

You:

1. _____

2. _____

3. _____

21

Three things I would like to accomplish
with you this year are:

Me:

1. _____

2. _____

3. _____

22

One adventure I am looking forward to with you is...

You:

_____

_____

_____

_____

_____

_____

_____

_____

_____

_____

_____

22

*One adventure I am looking
forward to with you is...*

Me:

_____

_____

_____

_____

_____

_____

_____

_____

_____

_____

My hopes and dreams for our future as a couple are...

You:

_____

_____

_____

_____

_____

_____

_____

_____

_____

_____

_____

_____

*My hopes and dreams for our
future as a couple are...*

Me:

_____

_____

_____

_____

_____

_____

_____

_____

_____

_____

_____

Do you feel like you deserve me?
Why or why not?

You:

_____

_____

_____

_____

_____

_____

_____

_____

_____

_____

24 *Do you feel like you deserve me?*
Why or why not?

Me:

_____

_____

_____

_____

_____

_____

_____

_____

_____

_____

_____

25

Because of you, I discovered...

You:

_____

_____

_____

_____

_____

_____

_____

_____

_____

_____

_____

Because of you, I discovered...

Me:

_____

_____

_____

_____

_____

_____

_____

_____

_____

_____

_____

26

*One thing about our differences
that I cherish the most is...*

You:

_____

_____

_____

_____

_____

_____

_____

_____

_____

_____

_____

26

*One thing about our differences
that I cherish the most is…*

Me:

_____

_____

_____

_____

_____

_____

_____

_____

_____

_____

I feel loved by you when you...

You:

1. _____

2. _____

3. _____

4. _____

5. _____

6. _____

7. _____

8. _____

9. _____

10. _____

27

I feel loved by you when you...

Me:

1. _____

2. _____

3. _____

4. _____

5. _____

6. _____

7. _____

8. _____

9. _____

10. _____

I smile when I think about our relationship because...

You:

_____

_____

_____

_____

_____

_____

_____

_____

_____

_____

_____

_____

I smile when I think about our relationship because...

Me:

_____

_____

_____

_____

_____

_____

_____

_____

_____

_____

_____

29 The things I would like to do more
of and less of this year are...

You:

_____

_____

_____

_____

_____

_____

_____

_____

_____

_____

_____

29

The things I would like to do more of and less of this year are...

Me:

_____

_____

_____

_____

_____

_____

_____

_____

_____

_____

_____

30

The most important thing I have done in my life so far is...

You:

_____

_____

_____

_____

_____

_____

_____

_____

_____

_____

30 *The most important thing I have done in my life so far is...*

Me:

_____

_____

_____

_____

_____

_____

_____

_____

_____

_____

_____

31

This is how I feel when we talk about sex...

You:

_____

_____

_____

_____

_____

_____

_____

_____

_____

_____

_____

31

This is how I feel when we talk about sex...

Me:

_____

_____

_____

_____

_____

_____

_____

_____

_____

_____

_____

32

You can tell me no without hurting my feelings by...

You:

_____

_____

_____

_____

_____

_____

_____

_____

_____

_____

32

You can tell me no without
hurting my feelings by...

Me:

_____

_____

_____

_____

_____

_____

_____

_____

_____

_____

_____

33

These are some things I approach differently because of you...

You:

_____

_____

_____

_____

_____

_____

_____

_____

_____

_____

_____

These are some things I approach differently because of you...

Me:

_____

_____

_____

_____

_____

_____

_____

_____

_____

_____

34 *What makes you different from everyone is...*

You:

_____

_____

_____

_____

_____

_____

_____

_____

_____

_____

34

What makes you different from everyone is...

Me:

_____

_____

_____

_____

_____

_____

_____

_____

_____

_____

_____

35

This is how I would summarize our love story:

You:

_____

_____

_____

_____

_____

_____

_____

_____

_____

_____

_____

_____

35

This is how I would summarize our love story:

Me:

_____

_____

_____

_____

_____

_____

_____

_____

_____

_____

_____

36

These are five ways I love being physically intimate with you:

You:

1. _____

2. _____

3. _____

4. _____

5. _____

36

These are five ways I love being physically intimate with you:

Me:

1. _____

2. _____

3. _____

4. _____

5. _____

37 One lesson in life I wish I had learned sooner is...

You:

_____

_____

_____

_____

_____

_____

_____

_____

_____

_____

_____

37

One lesson in life I wish I had learned sooner is...

Me:

_____

_____

_____

_____

_____

_____

_____

_____

_____

_____

38

Talking about money with you makes me feel...

You:

_____

_____

_____

_____

_____

_____

_____

_____

_____

_____

38

Talking about money with you makes me feel...

Me:

_____

_____

_____

_____

_____

_____

_____

_____

_____

_____

_____

_____

39

If there were no consequences, I would love to...

You:

_____

_____

_____

_____

_____

_____

_____

_____

_____

_____

_____

39

If there were no consequences, I would love to...

Me:

_____

_____

_____

_____

_____

_____

_____

_____

_____

_____

_____

_____

_____

I feel respected by you when...

You:

_____

_____

_____

_____

_____

_____

_____

_____

_____

_____

_____

40

I feel respected by you when...

Me:

_____

_____

_____

_____

_____

_____

_____

_____

_____

_____

_____

 On a scale of one to ten, with ten being the highest, this is how I would rate my self-esteem, and why:

You:

_____

_____

_____

_____

_____

_____

_____

_____

_____

_____

_____

 On a scale of one to ten, with ten being the highest, this is how I would rate my self-esteem, and why:

Me:

_____

_____

_____

_____

_____

_____

_____

_____

_____

_____

_____

*These are five ways I feel connected
to you emotionally:*

You:

1. _____

2. _____

3. _____

4. _____

5. _____

42

These are five ways I feel connected
to you emotionally:

Me:

1. _____

2. _____

3. _____

4. _____

5. _____

You matter so much to me because...

You:

_____

_____

_____

_____

_____

_____

_____

_____

_____

_____

You matter so much to me because...

Me:

_____

_____

_____

_____

_____

_____

_____

_____

_____

_____

What I usually listen for when we have a conversation is...

You:

_____

_____

_____

_____

_____

_____

_____

_____

_____

_____

 **44**

What I usually listen for when we
have a conversation is...

Me:

_____

_____

_____

_____

_____

_____

_____

_____

_____

_____

_____

_____

Five things I want to try with you
when it comes to sex are:

You:

1. _____

2. _____

3. _____

4. _____

5. _____

Five things I want to try with you
when it comes to sex are:

Me:

1. _____

2. _____

3. _____

4. _____

5. _____

46 *Some of my favorite memories of us are...*

You:

_____

_____

_____

_____

_____

_____

_____

_____

_____

_____

_____

_____

Some of my favorite memories of us are...

Me:

_____

_____

_____

_____

_____

_____

_____

_____

_____

_____

_____

47   *Five things we have in common are...*

You:

1. _____

2. _____

3. _____

4. _____

5. _____

47

Five things we have in common are...

Me:

1. _____

2. _____

3. _____

4. _____

5. _____

The happiest you have made me so far is...

You:

_____

_____

_____

_____

_____

_____

_____

_____

_____

_____

_____

The happiest you have made me so far is...

Me:

_____

_____

_____

_____

_____

_____

_____

_____

_____

_____

_____

49

I want my legacy to be...

You:

_____

_____

_____

_____

_____

_____

_____

_____

_____

_____

49

I want my legacy to be...

Me:

_____

_____

_____

_____

_____

_____

_____

_____

_____

_____

50

I never want you to forget...

You:

_____

_____

_____

_____

_____

_____

_____

_____

_____

_____

50 *I never want you to forget...*

Me:

_____

_____

_____

_____

_____

_____

_____

_____

_____

_____

_____

It's so romantic when you...

You:

_____

_____

_____

_____

_____

_____

_____

_____

_____

_____

51

It's so romantic when you...

Me:

_____

_____

_____

_____

_____

_____

_____

_____

_____

_____

_____

52 *Three simple daily habits I can maintain to enhance our relationship are:*

You:

1. _____

2. _____

3. _____

52 *Three simple daily habits I can maintain to enhance our relationship are:*

Me:

1. _____

2. _____

3. _____

Thank You

Congratulations on completing this book. We hope it has opened up some dialogue and strengthened your relationship.

If you enjoyed using this book, please leave us a review on Amazon and share the book with other couples. You can even gift this book to your friends and family.

To receive email updates about future books, courses, and more, visit our website below and join our book fan community today:

www.ourpeacefulfamily.com/bookfan

Thank you again for choosing and using this activity book.

Ash and Marcus Kusi

Other Books by Ash and Marcus

Our Bucket List Adventures: A Journal for Couples

Quizzes for Couples: Fun Questions to Complete Together and Strengthen Your Relationship

Our Love Story Journal: 138 Questions and Prompts for Couples to Complete Together

Questions for Couples: 469 Thought-Provoking Conversation Starters for Connecting, Building Trust, and Rekindling Intimacy

Our Gratitude Journal: 52 Weeks of Love, Mindfulness, and Appreciation for Couples

Love Notes From Me to You: A Fun and Personalized Book With Prompts to Fill Out

About the Authors

Ash and Marcus help overwhelmed newlyweds adjust to married life, and inspire married couples to improve their marriage so they can become better husbands and wives.

They do this by using their own marriage experience, gleaning wisdom from other married couples, and sharing what works for them through their website and marriage podcast, *The First Year Marriage Show*.

Visit this website to listen to their podcast: www.firstyearmarriage.com

To learn more about them, visit: www.ourpeacefulfamily.com

Marriage is a lifelong journey that thrives on love, commitment, trust, respect, communication, patience, and companionship.

—Ashley and Marcus Kusi

Made in the USA
Las Vegas, NV
04 October 2022

56564992R00070